HOW TO BE THE BEST WRITER EVER!

AN INFORMAL GUIDE AND SOURCE OF INSPIRATION FOR NEW AND NOT SO NEW WRITERS WORLDWIDE

FAY KNOWLES

Cover image: Cape Santa Maria Beach,
Long Island, Bahamas
Copyright © 2018 Fay Knowles

Updated Cover Design with Writer on Beach:

Sam Aalam

Formatting:

Michael Davie
https://www.grimhousepub.com/

Photography:

Gavin Knowles

ISBN-10 : 1725510855

ISBN-13 : 978-1725510852

(Content updated February, 2021. Cover updated March, 2021.)

CONTENTS

ABOUT THE AUTHOR

FAY KNOWLES is a Scottish-born author who made The Bahamas her home many years ago.

She has been writing since the age of nine, penned a children's adventure book at eleven and won a school essay competition at age fifteen.

After leaving school at sixteen, she trained in Devon, England, as a secretary, then newspaper reporter. At the age of twenty she set off to "work her way around the world", first emigrating by ship to Canada.

She worked as an editorial assistant for the former Canadian Food Journal and Gift Buyer, Toronto. And then, to avoid a Canadian winter and to seek sunnier climes, she took a Greyhound coach down across the U.S. from Toronto to Miami, en route for The Bahamas.

She met her future husband Erskine in Nassau a month after that and they were married the following year. She jokes: "I never did travel the world"!

As well as getting by-lines in British and Bahamian newspapers, Fay's articles have appeared in Westward News (a former in house publication of British Telecom), the Kennel Gazette (official journal of the British Kennel Club), Christian Herald, and Sports Magazine Bahamas.

Her writing assignments have included articles for Bahamas Information Services, travel writing for Royal Caribbean Cruise Lines, and as a photo journalist for a shopping mall in Nassau, Bahamas. She once worked as a secretarial "temp" for the late Sir Etienne Dupuch, former Publisher/Editor of The Tribune, Nassau, transcribing his long, captivating editorials.

Fay's short stories have been published in The Lady magazine, England, and The Broadkill Review, USA; with poetry in the British magazine Evergreen.

The author drew on her Scottish background and knowledge of The Bahamas when writing her novel "Dangerous Devotion" (formerly "Love at Sunset"), Book One in her Buchanan Mystery Romance Series. And her mini-memoir "The Scottish Connection: A Journey Back" tells of her journey back to Scotland with her mother and young sons to revisit their Scottish roots.

Connect with Fay at https://fayknowles.blogspot.com

DEDICATED to all my loyal readers out there who have picked up a newspaper or magazine with my stories, articles or poems in them, read my blog or newsletters, followed me on social media, or bought my books. Thank you! You have made it all worthwhile!

INTRODUCTION

My son Gavin once said to me, "Mum, with all the years you have been writing, you should share your writing knowledge with others." And this is what I have tried to do with this book.

I don't have a university degree and don't know absolutely everything about writing, of course. However, I once trained as a newspaper reporter and have had many years of experience in the writing field, with disappointments as well as triumphs. And we can all learn from our pitfalls!

Included in this writer's guide are tips to thrust you forward as a writer - some for books, some for poetry, some for short stories or articles, a few for screenplays and some incorporating all of those together.

You can go as far as you want if you keep studying your craft and work hard at becoming a successful writer. One day your words will live on in eternity, where readers will treasure what you have written.

CHAPTER 1
BECOMING A WRITER

WHEN I first came to The Bahamas from the UK via Canada and the United States in 1965, I was twenty-one years old and had been writing since I was nine. – No, I don't mind giving away my age! That's the beauty of being a writer. You can write well into your "senior" years and no one can ever fire you!

My fascination with books started when I was hardly more than a toddler. My Scottish granny sometimes allowed me into the library of the old listed house where my grandfather worked on his employers' Stirlingshire estate. I'd attempt to read the words in the leather bound books, but my vocabulary was limited and the print too fine.

Then when I was nine years' old I read a poem about a babbling brook that inspired me to start writing. I had discovered my passion! I couldn't stop writing.

At eleven years old I wrote a children's adventure book in an old shop ledger of my father's. That ledger went with me everywhere while I was writing the book, so I could scribble the story in every spare minute – school recesses, lunch hours, after school instead of playing with my friends.... I finished the book, but sadly, it was later lost in my travels. I do have a few pages of the book that my mother transcribed into more legible writing for me when I was still a child, so perhaps I'll be able to jump-start the book again one day.

Beating all odds

It wasn't easy for me to become a "real" writer. When I was fourteen years old, my mother went to the headmistress of my school and told her: "Fay wants to be a writer." The head-mistress replied: "Fay will never be a writer!" However, since then I won a school essay competition; I became a newspaper reporter; my short stories and poetry have been published in print and digital magazines; my articles have appeared in magazines, journals, the British press and Bahamian newspa-pers; I have written on assignment for Royal Caribbean Cruise Lines, cruising the Caribbean on the former "MS Sovereign of the Seas"; I've worked as a Photo Journalist for a shopping mall; and I've had books published on Amazon!

I beat all odds – and you can too!

The challenges

I left school at the age of sixteen because that's what girls often had to do in those days. I only passed five British GCE "O" Levels (two the first time and then three more at my second attempt).

For some crazy reason I had thought I would pass all ten without even studying! Of course, I didn't want studying to interfere with my writing plus it was a fantastic summer that year. I spent what should have been study time, sunbathing, writing and reading in the garden!

My career choices were limited as a young woman then. I could have trained to become a teacher, physiotherapist, airline stewardess, nurse – or joined the Navy! But what I really wanted to do was to work for a newspaper and train as a reporter "from the bottom up".

I didn't mind covering just flower shows to start with! However, only boys were accepted to work and train in our local newspaper at the time and my mother would not allow her only child to move to London at such a "tender age" to become a journalist!

Learning the basic skills

Mum insisted I train as a secretary, saying I could always use the shorthand and typing for my writing (she was right – aren't mothers always right?!). I obeyed and took a one year secretarial course at Technical College, where I discovered I loved and excelled in shorthand and typing - probably because they are forms of communication and communication is part of my psyche as a writer!

I also studied commerce and basic law. What I learned about law has stood me in good stead throughout my working life, both in my secretarial jobs and with my writing.

After successfully completing my secretarial course, I took a job as secretary to the Welfare Officer of St. Loyes College for the Disabled, Exeter, Devon. I thought it would be more interesting than the bank job that was offered to me. And it was! I soon became captivated with the everyday lives of the students.

Becoming a newspaper reporter

I finally had my chance to train as a reporter when two former London Fleet Street journalists started a news agency in my town. They took me on as a "Girl Friday". This meant I not only received intense training as a reporter from two of the best in the business, but they also sent me to day release classes at the local college with boys from the same newspaper that wouldn't take me on! Back in the news agency's office I also had to do some secretarial work and make the coffee!

As a rookie reporter, my mentors sent me out on some challenging assignments. Once I covered a murder case, dragging the agency's photographer along with me. My favourite stories, however, were features, such as locating needy families at Christmas that a national newspaper wanted to present with turkeys.

Another time I had to cover a rugby match. I didn't have the foggiest idea about the sport, so I took a friend with me, to give a step by step summary of what was going on. I scribbled his comments in my notebook and turned in quite a decent story.

As this was before the advent of the Internet, I had to telephone my stories into the national newspapers on a daily basis.

Since my stint as a newspaper reporter I have continually written and studied my craft throughout life, including while bringing up our two sons. I have also used my skills as a qualified secretary to work at a variety of interesting jobs over the years. These often provided me with ideas or content for my writing. Unfortunately, most struggling writers must have a "day job"!

When to start writing

You may be like me, starting to write at nine years' old.

Or you may be like Laura Ingalls Wilder, born in 1867. She didn't start writing her "Little House" book series until 1932 when she was sixty-five years old!

It doesn't matter at what time in your life you start to write; what's important is that when you do, you commit yourself to writing the very best you can.

You too can be a successful writer if you have a passion for writing, a desire for excellence and are willing to put in many hours of hard work.

CHAPTER 2
THE WHO, WHAT, WHERE, WHEN, WHY AND HOW OF WRITING

WHO to write for?

Select your target audience – young; old; trendy; traditional; scholastic; romantic. Aim your pen or your computer keys at your chosen readers. Study the markets and get your work off to a publisher or publication.

WHAT to write?

"Write what you know" and "write what you like" – but most importantly, write FOR YOUR READERS.

In the beginning I wrote poetry, pages and pages of it. And I never went a day without making an entry in my diary. I also scribbled endless tales of horror, mystery, deceit and romance. I enjoyed everything I wrote, but I didn't submit it anywhere, so nothing was published! I just lived in my own little world of writing and shoved my work away in a drawer.

Then I started to write FOR MY READERS rather than just for my own pleasure. I studied my craft, submitted my work and I began to be published.

Some authors love the sound of their own "voice" and ramble on and on. Readers will get bored if you don't get to the point.

We must always write for our readers, not ourselves.

WHERE to write

As a child, my special places to write were high on the sturdy branches of an old oak tree or on a yellow blanket of primroses beside a river. Later, as a working mother, I used a credenza in our living room. This held my writing material, magazines and books. It opened up with a writing surface but my work could be locked away from prying little fingers. I didn't even own a typewriter then. I typed my stories in lunch breaks at work.

My home office computer is now my main "place" to write. Occasionally, I still scribble draft stories and articles in a steno pad.

I kick myself if I'm stuck in traffic and don't have a pen and pad. It's a great opportunity to write a few paragraphs of your latest work in progress. Don't forget to put your work away though when the traffic starts moving!

Doctors' and dentists' waiting rooms are also good places for writing. They're usually quiet and the other patients normally too preoccupied with their visit to notice you biting your pen in deep thought. Of course, nowadays many people use their phone or other mobile device when they get ideas.

Years ago I was stuck in a broken elevator for an hour on my own after leaving the office. Not only did I have no one to talk to, I had no pen and no paper to write on. What a waste of writing time! However, I did write about the experience afterwards. The article was published in my company's in house magazine and I got paid for it.

Long flights or airport delays are golden opportunities too for elaborating on your work in progress. Relaxing on a hot, sunny beach with notepad and pen may also be quite productive, but your paper can get a bit sticky with sand and sea spray!

Many writers use a garden shed for their writing place; others a closet or hallway. Bestselling author the late Mary Higgins Clark said she wrote at her kitchen table as her five children were growing up. Some really lucky writers have a den or office of their own to write in. Of course, what writer wouldn't revel in a house with an ocean view and your own hammock to swing in as you type away on your laptop?!

WHEN to write

Some writers are early risers and work from dawn to noon; others write dawn to dusk; and some write when they get home from their "day job", often into the "wee" hours.

Choose the time when you are most relaxed and your creativity is at its peak. There's no point in rushing to complete a writing project between the demands of your family or job. Wait until you have a quiet moment alone. You can achieve more in short spurts of quiet creativity than in long periods of chaos.

WHY write

Have a desire to write

You must WANT to write! "Real" writers love to create believable characters; set descriptive scenes; move readers to tears or laughter; or inform the uninformed.

See your work in print

To see your work in print for the first time is like the joy of birth or discovering that very special person in your life is in love with you!

Unfortunately, after my first short story acceptance decades ago, I never saw it in print. I'd heard about a possible market for short stories at one of my writers' club meetings. It was a tyre magazine of all things!

Afterwards we all rushed home to submit something to them. Mine was a satirical piece of fiction about a dentist. Somewhat foolishly at the time, I signed away all rights to the story.

I was overjoyed when I received a letter from the magazine, enclosing a cheque and saying that my story had been accepted. I'd had many articles published over the years, but this was my first short story acceptance.

However, despite repeated requests for a copy of the magazine where my story appeared, I had no response from them. I have a feeling they might have used my story to distribute to markets around the world.

That trade magazine is no longer in operation, but I always imagine my story could be out there somewhere, floating around like a lost child, while someone receives royalties from it!

Lesson: Never sign away all rights to your work unless you don't mind saying goodbye to it forever!

It's an escape

We all go through ups and downs in life. When pressures of family or work send you into despair, take up your pen or go to your computer and write.

You can make money at it

We can't all write full time. Most of us must have a steady income from a "day job" to pay our bills or support our family. However, if you study your craft there are many ways you can make extra money from writing:

- Study the markets and submit your short stories, poems, screenplays or articles to suitable publications or film companies.
- Write books and self-publish.
- Get paid for writing press releases, copy writing, ghost writing or editing.
- Write a regular column for one of your local newspapers.
- Search online for calls for writers.

You can help others

I usually expect to be paid for my writing. That validates me as a writer. However, I often feel drawn to help others, who do not have the resources to pay me for my writing. For example:

- I once wrote a story about a young hard working single mother who lost her house in a fire, to help raise funds to rehouse her.
- I wrote and sent out a press release about an amazing young man with a disability, to promote the books he had written.
- I covered a musical event, held to raise money for a group of very talented children so they could obtain violins for their orchestra, and wrote about it.
- I wrote an article for the newspapers about the importance of donating blood to our local hospitals.

It's a wonderful feeling to give back in some small way with our God given writing talent.

HOW to write

I don't profess to have all the answers to this age old question, but I will try to offer a little advice from my own experience.

Style

For centuries, students have been instructed how to write correctly, but writing STYLE cannot be taught. Your own personal style comes with practice.

A few basic tips

- Grab your reader at the very beginning (the "hook"). Keep the plot or story moving along quickly. If you don't they will quickly lose interest.
- Make sure you have a beginning, middle and end in the story.
- Often "less" is better than "more". If you are struggling with a sentence or paragraph, sometimes the piece will read much better if you just remove it.
- Don't name your characters with similar names or even the same first letter in their names. This can confuse readers. I often have to go back and re-read parts of a book to see who is doing what!
- If real people are mentioned in a non-fiction piece, get their permission first before including their names and/or photos.
- Don't use real people in your works of fiction. You could get sued!
- Don't leave any loose ends or your reader will feel cheated.

- Don't clump too much dialogue together in your fiction. For example, insert descriptions, senses, settings or action here and there. The same with exposition. Give some relief by scattering a little dialogue, etc. throughout the piece.
- Make an article more interesting by sprinkling a few quotes amongst the text.
- It's not necessary any more to insert two spaces between sentences (like I learned in secretarial college!). One space is now acceptable.
- Use active verbs and avoid using adverbs. If you say: "He cheerfully smiled at her" - you don't need the adverb "cheerfully" as the sentence already states he smiled, which indicates that he is cheerful! Take it out and just say: "He smiled at her".
- Avoid long run-on sentences in your fiction, e.g. "Justin drove up to the night club, parked in the car park and looked for his friends, who were supposed to meet him there, but he didn't see them anywhere, so he got back into his car and drove home." Ouch! That sentence is too long, clumsy and drawn out. Instead, you could say: "Justin drove up to the nightclub and parked in the car park. His friends were supposed to meet him, but he didn't see them anywhere. He got back into his car and drove home." Not the most elegant and descriptive writing, but you get what I mean?
- Avoid little used and little known words that send your reader running to their dictionary all the time. Keep language simple - unless you are writing a scholastic textbook of course!
- Avoid passive words. You can use a Thesaurus to find better words that have the same or nearly the same meanings. For example, further on in this book I was going to say "come to mind" in one of my sentences.

That was too passive, so I changed it to "spring to mind". See the difference?!

- Be creative with your character descriptions. In my novel "Dangerous Devotion" (formerly "Love at Sunset"), I could have said: "Violet's eyes were a brilliant Irish blue and she had very little grey in her hair. She was descended from colonial ancestors." – and - "Gordon had silver white hair." Instead, I say: "Her eyes a brilliant Irish blue, Violet's colonial genes had endowed her with very little grey, unlike Gordon with his abundance of silver white."

- All good fiction should have a theme running through it.

- To plot or not to plot? It's entirely up to you. You might like to write your book "from the seat of your pants", rather than plotting the book first. I did that with my first novel, but by the time I got about a third of a way through the book I started losing track of the time sequence and which characters were doing what and when! At that point I had to do a quick summary of the plot to sort everything out.

- Never end by saying it was all a dream! That's a cop-out (easy way out)!

- And remember the old adage SHOW DON'T TELL!

Take up your pen or place your fingers on your computer keys. Keep studying your craft, keep writing and YOU can become a writer!

CHAPTER 3
NEVER TOO OLD

YOU'RE never too old to learn – or to write! I successfully completed a Novel Writing Course when I was fifty years old (after I'd already "graduated" from a Short Story Writing Course) and I'm continually looking for ways to improve and market my writing.

Here are a few tips on how to jump-start the writing habit whatever your age:

Subscribe to a writing magazine

"Writer's Digest" magazine was my writer's "bible" for many years. When I'd open my post office box and spot the latest edition peeping out at me, I'd rip it out of its brown envelope like a small child tearing open a present. It's full of helpful writing tips and informative articles, as well as inspiring stories of writers' achievements.

Unfortunately, my copies of WD kept "disappearing" en route to our post office box in Nassau (we don't have postal deliveries to street addresses here)! Now you can subscribe to digital issues of WD.

There are many other writing magazines on the market. Just do a search on the Internet.

Browse a book store

Scan the shelves of writers' books for new study material and check out the different sections, to see what is currently popular in your genre.

I don't bring books back in my suitcase any more when travelling abroad, as I made that mistake on one of my trips to the UK. My suitcase was so heavy, I injured my hip and arrived back in The Bahamas in a wheel chair (don't worry; I recovered!).

Now if I can't find a book in one of our local bookstores, I special order it or order the book online.

Join a book club

Many service clubs, private organizations and individuals start their own book clubs.

Check out the Internet or your local library for a book club near you.

Attend a workshop

Writers' workshops can be found online as well as being held at physical locations.

Take a writing course

Sign up for one of the many writers' courses that are advertised in writing magazines or online. I obtained my Certificates in

Novel Writing from Writer's Digest School and in Short Story Writing from International Correspondence School in the days when study material went back and forwards between tutor and student via the postal system.

Now there are many writers' courses on the web. Also, don't forget the writing courses offered by your local college.

Keep a journal

It is said that keeping a journal helps to harness your creativity. Many writing tutors stress this to their students.

Get help from your peers

You can learn a lot from fellow members of a writers' group, listening to excerpts of their work and discussing writing in general. These groups often have guest speakers as well. See the chapter "Writers' Groups".

Enter some writing contests

There are many writing contests out there. Some require an entry fee. I avoid those with fees, as there are plenty of others that are free to enter! However, some of the contests with entry fees are quite prestigious, so they might be worth entering. That's your personal choice if you can afford it.

Use your local library

Take advantage of the facilities offered by your local library. Study quietly at your leisure.

Surf the web

The Internet has opened up a whole new world of learning. If you don't have your own computer or Internet access there are many places where this is offered. See the chapter "The Internet".

Get personal

Form your own personal study methods. I tick book chapters, stories and articles as I read them, so I don't waste time at a later date rereading - unless I particularly want to refer back to a specific article or section of the book. In that case, I "flag" the item, indicating the content on a small sticky piece of paper, so it's easy to locate at a later date.

Just do it!

Make the time to learn and advance yourself as a writer. Above all, JUST DO IT! You're never too old to learn.

CHAPTER 4
IDEAS

I ARRIVED in The Bahamas in 1965. My plan had been to work my way around the world and write about all my interesting experiences. I knew I would get an abundance of ideas for my stories, poems, articles and books.

I'd travelled to Canada by ship, worked as an editorial assistant at the former Canadian Food Journal and Gift Buyer for a few months, and then with winter approaching, decided to move somewhere warmer.

My uncle's secretary suggested: "Why not try The Bahamas?"

"The Bahamas?" I asked. "Where is that?!"

I turned the pages of my atlas. "Oh, you mean those little 'dots' off the Florida coast?!"

That sounded like a good plan. I would work in Nassau for three months, head back to England for Christmas (my mother had made me promise to be back by December!), and then try to find a friend who would accompany me working my way east as far as Japan!

I found out the cheapest way to get to The Bahamas was by Greyhound coach down across the USA from Toronto to Miami and then fly Bahamas Airways (as Bahamasair used to be called) to Nassau. United States Immigration let me in as I had an airline ticket out of there to Nassau, and Bahamas Immigration let me in as I had a plane ticket back to the USA. It would not be that easy today!

I arrived in Nassau on a Monday, found my job on the Tuesday and was granted a work permit on the Wednesday! The Bahamas was a British Colony at the time. It's an independent Commonwealth country now.

I met my husband a month after reaching Nassau, we were married the following year and I never did work my way around the world! I did go back to England that first Christmas, as I had promised my mother, but quickly returned to The Bahamas where Erskine proposed.

Today I look back at the adventures I've had over the years and ideas often pop up in my head for stories or articles.

I'd kept a journal during my travels; in fact I'd always kept a diary ever since I was a young child. This is a good source for ideas. Nowadays I must confess that I don't have time to keep a journal, but I am writing so much all the time, I think that suffices!

Where do writers get their ideas?

It's actually simpler than you think. All you need to do is be alert, be curious - and say to yourself "what if?"

Some of the places ideas can spring from

Newspaper articles

Ideas for short stories, articles or books can be found by scanning newspaper articles.

As an example, you may read an article about prison officials who are in deep trouble when they mistakenly set an inmate free long before his scheduled release date. What does this conjure up for a piece of fiction? Was he a murderer who goes on to kill again or was he wrongly accused with an opportunity now to prove his innocence?

Television headline news

You see a news report about a real estate agent with keys to a client's home finding the residents dead in bed. Idea for a story - does the realtor become implicated? Is she arrested? How does she prove her innocence?

Classified advertisements

Classified ads offer a wealth of ideas. In my youth, when I trained as a newspaper reporter, one of my daily duties was to read through the classifieds. Some successful stories came out of those ads. To this day, I still have a "nose for news". When I read about something unusual or informative in the classified columns, I cut it out and toss it into my "Ideas" file.

Movies

Sometimes a movie will set your mind on a new tangent. You cannot of course use the actual plot, theme, setting or characters from the movie, as that would be plagiarism. However, a multitude of ideas and new angles can result if you study how the writer has succeeded with the story.

Reading a book

Immerse yourself in a book. You might find yourself saying: "I could write something like that!" You wouldn't write the same story, of course, but reading stimulates the imagination and you can learn from how the plot develops.

A fleeting comment from a passer-by

A few simple words from a passer-by can send a writer's mind racing at full speed. Once I overheard a man talking on his phone about a death. It was probably quite innocent, but I saved it in my ideas file for future use!

Dreams

You can get ideas from your dreams. Keep a pen and paper next to your bed, to jot the dreams down when you wake up. As mentioned in Chapter Two though, never end a piece of fiction by saying it was all a dream!

Dreams don't just happen at night. Protagonists can start interacting in my imagination at any time of the day. Just leave your mind open to dream, dream, dream..... Don't do it when you're driving or operating machinery, of course!

Surfing the Internet

Take a ride through cyberspace and you will soon come up with ideas. All you need is time!

Once I found a site declaring they could make you an ordained minister of religion - for a fee, of course. Idea – a man who always wanted to become a priest purchases the "ordination" online and goes out in the world proclaiming he is now a minister of religion. What happens? Perhaps he forms his own church and actually becomes good at being a religious leader or maybe he gathers a group of gullible people around him and steals their money.

Personal experiences

Share your joys and triumphs, as well as disappointments. You can turn a negative experience into something positive. Write about it. It can earn you money and might be therapeutic for you.

On vacation

I write like crazy when I take a trip off the island, as there are always so many new sights and experiences. I also pick up lots of brochures and flyers to refer to later.

Court proceedings

Check out the courts. I wish I had time to sit through the multitude of court cases that we have in Nassau. I know I'd have the beginning of a book before the week was out!

Quotations

These can come from authors, poets, actors, statesmen, scientists, religious leaders, heroes, environmentalists or other persons of note.

Search "quotations" online or buy a book of quotations for a list of possibilities.

During a walk or jog

Walking or jogging stimulates the imagination. I listen to the birds singing, feel the breeze in my hair, look upwards at the ever-changing cloud formation, gaze at the pure beauty of trees and flowers or study the interaction of people around me. When I get back home I'm ready to let the pen or computer keys flow.

Everyday life

I live in a very "vibrant" neighbourhood! There's always something happening day or night.

Remember the classic movie "Rear Window", starring James Stewart and Grace Kelly, from Alfred Hitchcock's thriller about a wheelchair-bound photographer who witnesses a murder? If you keep your eyes and ears open to what's going on in your neighbourhood you might be able to come up with a similar (but different) plot!

Of course, I have very nice neighbours and I've never seen anyone in the vicinity who resembles a murderer (what does a murderer look like anyway?!), but put together a strange car parked outside in the early hours of the morning, its driver disappearing into the darkness, and you have the seeds of a plot!

What to do with your ideas

As you come up with ideas, store them somewhere, even if only on scraps of paper in a box or file. Better still, get them onto your computer as soon as possible, in a Word document under the heading "Ideas". Later, when you start working on a poem, article, story, screen play or book, you can look for topics, plots, themes, descriptions of characters, etc., in your collection of ideas.

If you store your ideas on a computer, make sure you back them up. Your ideas are invaluable, worth their weight in gold, and once lost, they are gone forever. In fact, back up all of your work on a regular basis. I continually back up work in progress onto a small jump drive that I keep on my key chain until that particular work is completed. But also, from time to time, I back up my main writing file on two backups (an external drive and another jump drive).

Of course, not all ideas come to fruition. You must be prepared to discard many of them later on!

CHAPTER 5
TIME MANAGEMENT

BACK in the '80s, living in Devon, England, I once had a job typing endless legal conveyances on a much used electric typewriter. Dina, another part-time secretary, was my daily companion in the dreary solicitor's office. I often wondered why she had little to say.

I'd try to make conversation, but my colleague typed solidly on, whisked her work away at the end of the morning and with a swift goodbye, headed home.

Some time later, when I no longer worked for the solicitor, I met her again, this time at a writers' club. We were all blown away when she read us portions of her eloquent stories.

Dina had several books published by traditional publishers and she was hoping to resurrect three of her paperbacks in large print. She was also very successful with magazine articles and stories. And while working as a tutor for a writers' correspondence school, she built up the number of her students to around one thousand.

We became good friends. She moved to Australia with her husband, her elderly mother and their dog, but we still kept in touch for many years. She wrote beautiful letters describing her new life down under.

I believe a major part of Dina's success was "Time Management". She went to the boring job every day (probably because she needed the money), but didn't waste any more time than she needed to. She did her work and got home quickly, to do what she most loved to do - write.

Organize your life (and make time for more writing!)

I used to think time management was only for personnel departments of large corporations. Then I purchased "How to Organize Your Life & Get Rid of Clutter", an audio cassette by Ab Jackson (Career Track Publications, Boulder, Colorado, USA). This helped to "declutter" my life and set me on the happy path to time management.

If you have a busy lifestyle - or even if you don't - "stuff" will often pile up. One tip that I remember from Ab Jackson's tapes and still put into practice is the "four box system". You'll probably find a way to use four or less or perhaps more boxes.

When I have a big "clear out", I enter a room armed with a box for charity, a box for garbage, a box for action, a box for items to keep and an electric shredder. I think the Ab Jackson system included a box for redirecting to other people.

I also take a pad, pen, stapler and staple remover with me. The pad and pen are for making notes of things that spring to mind as I am going through files or junk. The stapler and staple remover are for paperwork that needs to be associated or disassociated with a particular project or file.

Lists

Put business, personal and writing objectives into "to do" lists:-

1 = To be done that day
2 = To be done within the week
3 = To be done within a month

Store the lists on your computer or in note pads. As items on action lists 2 or 3 become more important, they're bumped up to the higher category.

Files

I find that "Pending" files are a waste of time. A decade ago, being executive secretary for a major wholesale and retail outlet + personal secretary for the CEO + the company's advertising coordinator, I had so much work and had to extend my desk to accommodate my growing number of "pending" files. I never did get to the end of them before I eventually quit the job!

Now, computers and the Internet can simplify your life. Create digital files instead of struggling with manila files in metal cabinets. Of course, don't forget to back up regularly!

Time Management Tips

- Be decisive. If you have a tedious project, tackle and complete it to the best of your ability, so you can get on with what you enjoy the most (in my case, writing!).
- Use your peak creativity period to write. Are you a morning or evening person? If you have a daytime job and are a "morning person", get up early and write

before breakfast; if you like to "burn the midnight oil", write in the evening.

- Telephone calls or visits from friends or relatives can prevent you from getting a story or article finished and sent off to a publisher. Gently encourage them to call first before stopping by. If you are busy when they telephone, let them know you are working to deadline and can you call them back. Also, friends or family members often make unnecessary demands on you. Learn to say "no" (within reason!).
- Group similar activities together and make a list when setting out on errands, planning your route, so you don't have to double back and waste time.
- Set priorities and goals, but remember, you don't have to be perfect!

John Keats, one of the top poets of his era, wrote he had "... fears that I may cease to be before my pen has glean'd my teeming brain....."

He lived from 1795 to 1821, dying at only 26 years old. If you don't take time in hand, your pen might not "glean your teeming brain"!

CHAPTER 6
WRITERS' GROUPS

INFORMATION on Writers' Groups is often posted in local libraries, published in writing magazines or displayed in bookstores. They can also be found online.

How to start a Writers' Group

If you don't have a Writers' Group in your area, why not start one? Run an ad in your local newspaper, place a notice in the library or invite new members via social media.

Meetings can be held in members' homes, in your favourite coffee shop or wherever is convenient for everyone. They can be as informal or formal as you wish.

Some writers' groups consist of people who only have a vague notion that they would like to write and others are made up of members who are more serious about their writing (or there could be a mixture of both).

When I belonged to the Exeter & District Writers' Club (now Exeter Writers) in Devon, England, we held the meetings in a community hall every third Saturday morning of the month. #1 New York Times Bestselling author the late Mary Higgins Clark once gave a talk to the Club. She inspired us so much that we all rushed home afterwards to get writing!

The Exeter club was run as many associations are, with appointments of officers and notices to members. Applications for membership in the Club had to include some published work and be approved by the Board. However, your writers' group can be just a casual meeting of friends or acquaintances.

Some years ago, I started an informal writers' group in Nassau by word of mouth. Then after the first little meeting in a café I sent out a press release to our local newspapers with photos of our gathering and how to contact me.

The group grew more and more with each subsequent press release, from about six people to around forty! We met once a month.

Eventually, the meetings became like writers' seminars! This required a lot of preparation by yours truly. It all became too much work on top of my "day job" and I had to bow out.

Sadly, no one else took over and the group closed down, but I truly believe the members benefited from the time it was in existence. And I enjoyed the writing fellowship.

I still love to get together with other writers, but these days we just meet for a coffee from time to time. No strings attached!

How to run a Writers' Group

It's up to you whether or not to charge a monthly or annual fee for membership in your writers' group. If it's just a small group and you have no overhead expenses, you may decide not to charge anything at all. However, if you pay guest speakers, rent a meeting place or have other club expenses, then a membership fee would be appropriate.

Don't forget to take into account the cost of any stationery or print cartridges you might use to print agendas, minutes or information from your home. And bear in mind you would be using your own electricity. Also, counter in the expense of refreshments you may provide.

When I ran the writers' group in Nassau, I didn't have to pay for the church room where we met, but I did eventually ask for small voluntary donations towards refreshments and stationery. Some members dropped a dollar or so in the pot and some didn't.

Ask members to share with the others any new markets they've recently discovered. Studying the markets is an imperative part of a writer's routine. And, of course, any recent writing successes should be announced at your meetings, with many congratulations and encouragement from everyone!

Each member should bring to the meeting something they wrote and read part of it for their fellow members' critique.

Readings should not be lengthy. You could ask one of your members to time each reading and let the person reading know when they have reached the set limit. Handouts of the work should be returned to the author after the reading.

You may not be particularly interested in another writer's chosen genre, but it's only courteous to listen attentively, just as you would want them to listen closely to what you've written.

After all, you may learn something, and that's a large part of what a writers' group is all about - sharing and learning.

Critiques should be constructive, not cruel! Be kind, positive and helpful.

As my dear old writer friend and mentor the late Jan Valpy, who invited me to join the Exeter and District Writers' Club, always said: "When you are doing a critique take care of the soul of the writer."

CHAPTER 7
OVERCOMING WRITER'S BLOCK

SOMETIMES what's happening in your day-to-day life can block your creativity – a car accident, houseguests or a family crisis, for example. The creative side of your brain becomes "stagnant" and frustration may set in, as you long for the peace and seclusion that will set your words dancing again!

I admire writers who continue to put pen to paper despite all odds, but everyone's not the same. Don't feel guilty if events in your life prevent you from writing. Once the intrusions or stressful situations have ceased, you'll bounce back again – and perhaps write some of your best work.

The many forms of writer's block

- Often we struggle with a sentence or word, moving it around in a paragraph and trying different ways to make it work.
- Sometimes we're bursting to get an idea down on paper; it seems like the beginning of a great story, then the flow of writing abruptly stops.
- Other times we are the middle of writing a story and it

comes to a screeching halt. We just can't think how to get it going again.

It's all due to that pesky teaser of the muse – "writer's block"!

Decades of writers have suggested methods for battling the "teaser". I feel the best line of defence is - don't despair and don't give in.

When a word or sentence doesn't work and you just can't think of an alternative, try leaving it out. Again, "less" is often better than "more".

If you have a great idea, put it down on paper immediately and if the writing flow stops, leave it for a while (even a day or so if necessary); go for a walk; spend time with your family or friends; read a book or watch a movie; and come back to it later.

Walking, jogging or other types of exercise not only take away the stress of the day, but activity also stimulates the brain cells.

The last thing you should do is panic! I know from experience that usually when I return to the piece, refreshed, everything starts to fall into place.

Tips to beat the pesky writer's block

- Put aside daily segments of time to write.
- Switch off the radio or television and just think, ponder, meditate.....
- Look through your "Ideas" file or journals for inspiration.
- Relax and listen to music.
- Sit in a public place and "people watch". Take in the sounds, smells and conversation around you.
- Browse a book store or library.

- Join a writers' group or online forum. Discuss your stumbling blocks with other writers, who are usually eager to come up with suggestions.
- If you're surrounded by "clutter", get rid of it. A "cluttered mind is not a productive mind". See the chapter "Time Management".
- Consider whether what you're writing is too biographical (unless it is a biography!). You may be subconsciously worrying that a friend or family member might recognize themselves or you in the story. If so, work on changing the background, setting, characters and circumstances (I assume you are not using real names, of course!).
- Sometimes you may be too "close" to the topic. Step back and look objectively at what you are trying to get across to your reader.

Above all, don't let that pesky teaser beat you!

CHAPTER 8
WRITERS' RESOURCES

NOWADAYS, there are many writers' resources. I often wonder how olden-time authors like Charles Dickens managed to be so prolific. Of course, they had so much more of that precious commodity we now claim to lack - "Time" - and they probably spent hours and hours amongst stacks of neatly bound books in cool, quiet libraries!

Below are some resources I've used that you might find helpful (don't worry if some eventually become out of print as other similar suggestions will pop up when you do an online search):

Books for Writers

"Travel Writing for Profit & Pleasure" by Perry Garfinkel.

"Plot" by Ansen Dibell ("Elements of Fiction Writing").

"The Writer's Digest Handbook of Short Story Writing" - Preface by Joyce Carol Oates.

"How to Write & Sell your First Novel" by Oscar Collier and Frances Spatz Leighton.

"Writing A – Z" by Kirk Polking.

"Writing the Block Buster Novel" by Albert Zuckerman.

"Writing the Novel from Plot to Print" by Lawrence Block.

"Characters & Viewpoint" ("Elements of Fiction Writing") by Orson Scott Card.

"Write Your Heart Out" by Rebecca McClanahan.

"Formatting & Submitting Your Manuscript" by Cynthia Laufenberg and the Editors of Writer's Digest Books.

"How To Publish and Promote Online" by M. J. Rose and Angela Adair-Hoy.

"Writer's Market" by Robert Lee Brewer.

"Writer's Market: The Internet Edition" by Kirsten Holm.

"Writers' and Artists' Yearbook" (A & C Black, London, England).

"The Writer's Handbook" by Barry Turner (Macmillan).

"Novel and Short Story Writer's Market" (Writer's Digest Books – F & W Publications).

"How to Write Poetry" by Paul B. Janeczko (Scholastic Guides).

Inspirational

"Chicken Soup for the Writer's Soul" by Jack Canfield, Mark Victor Hansen and Bud Gardner.

"Word by Word" by John Tullius & Elizabeth Engstrom and the presenters of the Maui Writers Conference.

English Grammar

It's good to have a basic little grammar guide on hand. You might find one of these does the job:

"The One Minute Grammarian" by Morton S. Freeman (Signet).

"The Everyday English Handbook" by Leonard Rosen (Doubleday).

"Good Grammar" by Graham King (Collins).

Of course, the Spell Check, Grammar and Thesaurus in Microsoft Word on your computer are helpful, as well as www.Thesaurus.com and www.Dictionary.com.

Miscellaneous

"Home Office Know-How" by Jeffery D. Zbar (Upstart Publishing).

"The New American Dictionary of First Names" by Leslie Dunkling & William Gosling (Signet) – this helps you come up with names for your characters!

"Roget's Thesaurus", first published by Peter Mark Roget in 1852. There are many versions of this most helpful collection of words with different or similar meanings. I often refer to it when I am grasping for words!

"Webster's Third New International Dictionary, Unabridged" by Merriam-Webster and Philip Babcock Gove.

"The Concise Oxford Dictionary of Current English" by H. W. Fowler and F. G. Fowler.

"National Geographic Atlas of the World" - Of course, any atlas should do.

Travel guides such as Fodor's - These help you check on a country's facts or give you background information for your descriptions when writing. The photos in travel guides can also give you the feeling of actually being where your story or article is set.

Local street maps – These help you imagine where your character is walking or driving or in the case of a non-fiction piece ensures you have a street's name spelled correctly.

History books – Imperative for research when going back in time, whether your book is fiction or non-fiction.

Department Store catalogues - Photographs of the models can spark descriptions of the characters in your story or book.

Books in the genre in which you wish to write - Study the author's techniques which brought about their success.

Youtube.com – This site has a lot of free tutorial videos on writing and publishing.

Magazines for Writers

"Writer's Digest" (F & W Publications, Ohio, USA).

"The Writer" (Madavor Media, Braintree, USA).

"Writing Magazine" (Warners Group).

Audio

"Writer's AudioShop" - www.writersaudio.com.

Libraries

Remember your local library for resources. You can spend hours in a public library, reading or writing, and no one dares disturb you!

Internet

To source the Internet, you don't have to be a computer "whiz" but you do need a little time. The web can open up a whole new world of information for you. See chapter "The Internet".

Writers' Groups

I am not normally a "joiner" of groups or organizations (I think most writers prefer their own company), but for motivation and information (as well as fellowship if you wish) I highly recommend you look for a good writers' group or start one yourself. The feedback and markets shared in these groups are invaluable. See chapter "Writers' Groups".

Writers' Workshops

The Maui Writers Conference, held annually in Hawaii. See the chapter "Writers' Resources": "Word by Word" by John Tullius & Elizabeth Engstrom and the presenters of the Maui Writers Conference (Writers House Books).

Writers' workshops are often advertised in the classified sections of writing magazines, listed in articles on the subject or promoted on the Internet.

Online workshops can also be found at the Writer's Digest University - writersonlineworkshops.com/

Writers' Courses

Writers' courses are available through reputable writing magazines or found by searching online.

Writers' Forums

Here are a couple (there are many others):

Romance Writers of America Community Forums (you have to be a member of RWA). Website: www.rwa.org

Writers Online - the Internet creative writing community from the publishers of "Writing Magazine" and "Writers' News" - www.writers-online.co.uk

Social Media

Unfortunately, a writer's life is not all about writing. We have to do our marketing too if we want our work to sell. Used sensibly, social media can be a great source of information and an opportunity to get yourself out there as a writer.

CHAPTER 9
THE INTERNET

WHY use the Internet?

The vast majority of you reading this will already be using the Internet (especially if you've downloaded the e-book editions of my books!) and you may be much more Internet savvy than I am.

It is so easy to communicate with writers near and far using the Internet, as well as with those editors who accept email submissions. And it is super fast to find information you need for your writing.

Our former family real estate business was one of the first in The Bahamas to have a real estate website. We couldn't have succeeded without it. And the same goes for my writing career.

The early days of the Internet

When I worked as PA to a British Telecom (BT) Board Member in the late eighties, I was sent by BT to Windsor, near London, for a short, intense Word Processing course. All this technology was very new to me; I had only just learned how to use a fax machine!

While on the course, we participants were taken to BT's London headquarters and shown the main computer system. This was where our messages to BT PAs in other regions would first land before being expedited to our colleagues' inboxes around the country (similar to the Internet, but a private network).

Of course, I took the opportunity to write about the Windsor experience. My article "Processed – Along with Joan Collins and a Smart Young Thing" appeared in BT's in house publication "Westward News" and later in The Tribune newspaper, Nassau, Bahamas, when we returned to the island. I was paid for both.

The tongue in cheek name "Joan Collins" referred to a very glamorous participant on the course, and the "Smart Young Thing" was just as the description implies – a smart young woman who was way ahead of me in technical ability!

I attended and received certificates for a total of three Word Processing Courses at Windsor, which gave me good grounding for the cyber world.

Can't live without it

How did we ever exist before The Internet?! Surf the web and you can find just about any information you're looking for, but be wise how you use it.

Like most, I am now quite dependent on the Internet! In the early days before the advent of smart phones, I always had to find an Internet café while travelling, because of our real estate business. I couldn't be without checking my email regularly on one of their computers, in case we missed a possible sale! I'd take my laptop on short trips, but found it was too cumbersome on long journeys.

Once I discovered Internet facilities in Oban, Scotland (Oban is a lovely little fishing port on the west coast). Their two computers were in the basement, next to the kitchen, with all the cooking smells and clatter that accompany it, but what a phenomenon at that time to email Nassau, Bahamas, from a cellar on the Scottish Seaboard!

Internet usage

I currently have two Facebook presences – one my personal page and the other my author page. I try to post nothing but positive comments. The same with my blog and other social media. I truly believe if you remain positive wherever you go on the Internet, you will continually be uplifted and will rarely encounter naysayers who might attempt to pull you down.

Domains

If you have your own web site, it can be "hosted" by an Internet hosting company. Some are more affordable than others. There's usually a monthly or annual fee, but you're often allowed one or more email addresses.

You too can purchase a domain name, in order to create your own website.

One of the companies you can buy a domain through is Network Solutions. Just go to their web site and insert the name of the domain you're interested in buying. Network Solutions will let you know whether or not it's available. Have your credit card ready and it can be yours for a small annual fee.

The next step is to design your website, using your domain name. You can buy software for this or pay someone to build it for you. Then launch your own website on the net.

Blogs are very popular now. My blog is currently https:// fayknowles.blogspot.com but if this changes, do an online search for my name.

And if you're not too computer literate, there are many basic books about computers and the Internet, or look for information online.

Pirated e-books

I was dismayed when I discovered that the e-book edition of my book "Sunbeams from the Heart – A Collection of Twelve Romantic Short Stories" was being pirated online!

I reported it to Amazon and they said: "I can confirm that we have not authorized these sites to loan your book and have not provided your file to them. If you have found your work available on an unauthorized website such as the sites that you referenced, we suggest contacting that website to confirm your rights and request removal of your work. If you distribute your book through other sales channels, you might contact them to inquire as to whether they have authorized the inclusion of your book on other sites. Our lending program allows a purchaser to lend a title once and does not allow the recipient to re-loan that book."

Unfortunately, it seems there's nothing much authors can do about it at this point in time. And people who access these pirate sites risk having their computer infected by viruses anyway.

I guess I could contact the "pirates" and ask them to cease and desist. Apparently this sometimes works for a while, but apparently it's not long before they start popping up again. And then there's the risk of getting a virus on my computer from these rogue sites.

Of course, the comparison has been made that our paperbacks can get passed around by being left on park benches, loaned to friends and donated to charity, without any compensation to the authors. I personally feel it's really not worth worrying about.

The Internet era

The Internet has advanced writers in a way that no other medium has ever done. When we put our work out there on the World Wide Web, it also increases our chances of a top publishing house or film director spotting our books and snapping them up!

CHAPTER 10
SUBMISSIONS

ONE of the keys to writing success is to keep submitting your work. It's tedious, I know. When that precious manuscript is returned to you with a curt rejection slip, in the stamped self-addressed envelope that you might have carefully weighed, stuck just the right amount of stamps on, put in another envelope and carried all the way to the post office, the last thing you want to do is start the process all over again!

Same thing when you receive a generic email response stating that a publication or publisher is unable to use your work (of course, since this book was written, email queries and submissions may have become the norm).

Nevertheless, if you continually submit to the markets, your reward can be your work in print when you least expect it and some nice cheques in the mail (or payment wired to your bank). I'm going to give you some rough guidelines, but keep checking your writers' handbooks, magazines and Internet resources for current trends.

Some book publishers request that you query first, so study the markets for submission guidelines before submitting. Also, safeguard yourself by researching the publisher before approaching them. You wouldn't want your precious work accepted by a publisher, only to discover later that their ethics were dubious or they went out of business. I'm always suspicious of publishers that have typos or out of date copyright notices on their websites.

Writers' forums can be useful for this. I often enter a publisher's name in their search box and it comes up with lots of threads, where other writers have been discussing that particular market. Of course, sometimes we just have to use our own gut feeling about a publisher, because warnings may have arisen out of a disgruntled author unhappy about their work not being accepted.

Multiple or simultaneous submissions

Multiple submissions should not be confused with simultaneous submissions. "Multiple" means submitting more than one manuscript to the same publisher or publication. "Simultaneous" means submitting the same manuscript to more than one publisher or publication.

Some publications or publishers don't want to see more than one manuscript (story, article or book) at a time from a writer. When submitting short stories or articles I don't have a difficulty with this, as I prefer to spread my work around. I feel this gives me more chance at acceptance. And with books, I am usually only working on one book at a time anyway.

There are a few publications and publishers who won't accept simultaneous submissions. In the case of short work, that's okay with me, as I like to wait until I hear back from them before sending the piece out again. My experience is that their response time is usually not that long, but if I don't hear back from them within a reasonable length of time I submit elsewhere. With some I might never hear back at all. Unfortunately, that's the name of the game!

With book publishers, however, I personally feel it's best to submit your work only to those who will accept simultaneous submissions, as it can take months to receive a reply from a publisher. Imagine how long you may be trying to find a publisher for your book if you only send it out to one publisher every three to six months? You could be submitting it for years!

Make sure you mention in your cover letter/email if this is in fact a simultaneous submission. It's also good to add that you will notify them immediately if your book is accepted elsewhere before you hear back from them. It is only fair to do so.

Submission Guidelines

Look for Submission (or Writers') Guidelines on the websites of publications or publishers. If they don't have a section "Submissions" you might find the information at "About Us", "Contact Us", or "Authors". If you have no luck with that, do a search online for the publication's submission (or writers') guidelines. Sometimes they will pop up in the results.

Examples of what Guidelines might state or request (not all at one time):

- Query first
- Whether to send by email or snail mail
- Word count for an article, story or book
- Number of lines for poetry
- Theme, genre or readers' age group
- Simultaneous submissions accepted or not
- Reading period

- Response time
- Attachments or enclosures
- Book submissions only through a literary agent

Follow the guidelines carefully. They vary a lot.

Querying by "snail" mail (postal delivery service) in advance of submissions if required

I haven't noticed any publications requiring queries for short stories or poems, but with feature stories/articles, books or screenplays this is sometimes the case.

When sending a short letter, pitching your idea, it's good to use the editor's name if you can locate it. However, if you can't find the current editor's name, just address the query "Dear Editor".

When using the editor's name, make sure you get it correct. If you really want to use an editor's name and can't find it in any of your resources, you can telephone their switchboard. To ask "What is the name of your editor?" is not infringing on privacy.

Head your letter with your name, address, phone number(s) and email address (plus web or blog address, etc., if you have them). See below under "Nuts and Bolts" for more information on letterhead.

With short stories or feature stories/articles, give the word count and genre. State briefly what your work consists of and give a little information about yourself. In the case of a feature story/article, tell the editor what inspired you to write it and why you feel you are qualified to write on this topic.

Your query letter should be brief (one page if possible). In the case of a book or screenplay, mention if the work is completed or not.

When sending a query, it's good to say IF this particular work has previously been published elsewhere. Personally, once one of my short stories or articles has been accepted and published I usually don't bother sending it out anywhere else, because I always have so many other new projects I'm working on. I'm just happy it found a home. But you can go ahead if you have the patience – and the time!

If you're not published yet, you might need to "sell" yourself. Don't draw attention to the fact you're unpublished though! And don't say things like "I am a really good writer" or "all of my friends tell me my stories should be published"! That reeks of inexperience. Tell the editor about any of your background experience that qualifies you to write about this topic or theme. Stick to the facts!

If photos or illustrations are available, mention in your query that these can be provided.

With all queries, mention any writing courses you've taken or writers' groups or writers' associations you belong to - anything you feel might give you more credibility. And of course, if you are already published, refer to those successes.

I usually sign a snail mail letter "Sincerely" and my name.

Enclose a standard business sized (#10) stamped self-addressed envelope (s.s.a.e.) for the editor's reply. Put "Air Mail" on the s.s.a.e. if you're targeting an overseas market; otherwise it might be returned by second class mail.

In the case of a book, very often a synopsis and a few chapters are required to accompany the query. Do not fold or staple your manuscript. Use paper clips. Send everything in a 9" x 12" envelope with another 9" x 12" s.s.a.e. envelope enclosed for return of the material if necessary.

Querying by email in advance of submissions if required

Fortunately, more and more publishers and publications are accepting queries and submissions by email. If you're querying by email, insert the query in the body of your email. Place the words "Query" and the title of your work in the subject line, unless the publisher's guidelines say otherwise. I often add my name as well ("by Fay Knowles"), as a publisher once said it was handy when searching emails for a particular author's work. Follow the guidelines above for snail mail queries, where appropriate.

If a publisher requires a synopsis and a few chapters with your query, attach them as Word attachments or copy and paste them into the body of your email (depending on their guidelines).

I sign off "Kind regards", my name, address, phone number(s), email and web links.

Submissions by "snail" mail

If you have been successful with your query or if a publisher or publication does not require that you query first, address your cover letter to the appropriate editor. If you can't find their name, again just say "Dear Editor".

If your submission is the result of a successful query, draw the editor's attention to this. Tell them about your work and include something short about yourself if you haven't done so previously. Again, follow submission guidelines for this.

Head your letter with your name, address, phone number(s) and email address (plus web or blog address, etc., if you have them).

Do not fold or staple your short stories, articles or poems. Use paper clips. Place your submission in a 9" x 12" envelope. In the event your work is not accepted and you want it returned, enclose a 9" x 12" stamped, self-addressed envelope (folded in half, to fit into the outer envelope).

If sending your book to a publisher by snail mail, the manuscripts should be submitted loose-leaf. If you wish, you can buy special manuscript boxes for this purpose.

If you have a copy of your work, it is also saved on your computer and you don't need it returned, let the editor know in your cover letter that your submission can be recycled if not accepted. In that case you only need to enclose a small #10 s.s.a.e. for their reply.

Postage when querying (or submitting) by snail mail overseas

When querying or submitting your work overseas, you will need that country's stamps for your s.s.a.e. As for postage on the envelope carrying your query or submission, I find it handy to keep a supply of local stamps (I have my own postal scales at home). Then you can put the correct amount of stamps on your envelopes and save long lines at the post office. When you travel abroad, pick up the current postal rates and a good selection of stamps from that overseas post office for future stamped self-addressed envelopes. You can also ask friends or relatives in foreign countries to send you a supply.

You can find United States postal rates at www.usps.gov.

For British postal rates go to www.royalmail.com.

Canadian rates are at www.canadapost.ca.

Many other countries' postal services can be found online.

Submissions by email

I suggest you put "Submission", the title of your work and by [your name] in the subject line, unless the submission guidelines say otherwise.

Say "Dear [and the editor's name]" or "Dear Editor" if you don't know their name. If your submission is the result of a successful query, draw the editor's attention to this. If not, tell them about your work and include something short about yourself. Again, follow submission guidelines for this.

Attach your story, poem, article or book manuscript, etc., as a Word doc, unless their submission guidelines say otherwise.

Sign off with "Kind regards", your name, address, phone number(s) and email (plus web addresses if you have any).

Reply cards for snail mail queries

You may receive a quicker response if you include a "reply" card with your snail mail query to publications and the editor might appreciate the fact you're trying to make the process easier for them. I rarely use reply cards any more myself, as my queries or submissions these days are by email, but you might find them useful.

Use a blank postcard or plain index card. Following is an example (you can print this on a self-adhesive label and stick it on one side of the card if you are unable to run it off on your printer):

Name of publication: [insert the name of the publication to whom you are addressing the query]

Author: [insert your name]

Title of story/article/script, etc: [insert the title of your work]

Date: [insert the mailing date]

Yes, we are interested in seeing [insert title of your work]: _______

[leave blank for them to tick!]

Sorry, we are not interested in [insert title of your work]: _______

[leave blank for them to tick]

(Please tick as applicable)

[directions for publication or publisher]

Comments [this is for the publication or publisher to hopefully complete]:

____

____

____

On the other side of the card, print your name and address, put enough stamps on the card for return postage, enclose it in the envelope with your query letter and sit back and wait!

Reply card for Snail Mail Submissions (similar to queries)

Use a blank postcard or plain index card. Following is an example (you can print this on a self-adhesive label and stick it on one side of the card if you are unable to run it off on your printer):

Author: [insert your name]

Title of story/article/script, etc: [insert the title of your work]

Date: [insert the mailing date]

Name of publication: [insert the name of the publication you are addressing the query to]

Yes, we accept [insert title of your work] for publication: _______

[leave blank for them to tick]

Sorry, we are unable to accept [insert title of your work]: _______

[leave blank for them to tick]

We are still considering [insert title of your work]: ________

[leave blank for them to tick]

(Please tick as applicable)

[directions for publication]

Comments: [this is for the publication or publisher to hopefully complete]

____

____

____

On the other side of the card, print your name and address, put enough stamps on the card for return postage, enclose it in the envelope with your submissions letter and sit back and wait!

Organizing your Writing files

I have a Big Writing Folder on my computer! I say "Big" because it contains everything to do with my writing. Following is how I organize my writing files, but you might have your own system. Whichever works for you is fine.

Submissions Record for books

Inside my Big Writing Folder, among many other folders and documents, I have a work folder for each of my books.

Inside the work folder for my first novel, I stored British publishers' and agents' submissions and American publishers' and agents' submissions, including manuscripts and synopses with British or American spelling; copies of my query or submission letters; information on each publisher or agent; their writers' guidelines, Submissions Record, etc.

The Submissions Record listed everywhere I sent the manuscript. I used a table grid that I set up in a Word doc. Some writers use Microsoft Excel.

I headed the Submissions Record page with the name of the book and in the columns I put the name of each publisher or agent I submitted the manuscript to, the date of submission, the date of their reply and the editor's comments if any.

Submissions Record for short stories & articles

Also in my Big Writing Folder, I have a Submissions Record folder for keeping track of my short stories and articles (and occasional poem). Each story/article also has its own individual Submissions Record sheet, listing everywhere I send the piece.

As with my book's Submissions Record, I use a table grid for each short story or article that I've set up in a Word doc. I head the Submissions Record page with the name of the piece. In the columns I put the name of each publication I submitted it to, the date of submission, the date of their reply, whether it was accepted or not, and the editor's comments if any. This way I can see at a glance where I have sent a story or article, how many times it has been submitted, etc.

I keep a General (Master) Submissions Record sheet inside the main Submissions Record folder, also with a table grid in Word, where I list all of my stories/articles/poems.

In one column I put the name of each piece, then in the other columns I add the name of the publication I submitted to, the date of submission, the date of their reply, whether it was accepted or not, and the editor's comments if any. It's not in alphabetical order, but I can always use "Edit/Find" to quickly locate a particular piece of work.

I print out a copy of this Submissions Records sheet from time to time, as an additional back up.

And this brings me to backing up! ....

Backing Up

Back up all of your work regularly. I keep a copy of my writing files not only on my computer, but I also back them up on an external drive and a flash drive (memory stick), which I keep in a safe (only documents are kept in our safe - no money!).

In addition, I usually back up whatever I'm working on at any particular time to a key chain memory stick every time I'm about to cut off my computer (and often as I go along).

The Nuts and Bolts of Submissions

Follow the guidelines of the publication or publisher you are submitting to. However, following are some general tips for snail mail submissions.

Paper

Use 8 ½" x 11" good quality white paper.

Print size

Usually 12 point Times New Roman. Double space, except for your name, address, etc.

Printers

Inkjet or laser printers are preferable.

Margins

1" to 1½" is usually acceptable.

Paragraphs

I use the Microsoft Word default indent of 0.5" for each first line of a paragraph, but some publishers' guidelines might require you to change that. In fact any of the above can have different specifications by a publisher. Again, make sure you read the submission guidelines carefully.

Cover letter design

This can be plain or at the top above your address you may insert a small logo that has relevance to your work.

Collating

Your cover letter should be separate. Use paper clips for the piece you're sending in, except with book manuscripts, which you should submit loose-leaf. As mentioned previously, if you wish, you can buy special manuscript boxes in which to ship your book to the publisher.

Short stories

Many handbooks advise: "Submit the complete manuscript without a cover letter." There's usually no need to query with a short story, but personally, I still think it's courteous to attach a brief cover letter with your submission.

Double space and use the Microsoft Word default indent of 0.5" unless otherwise specified in guidelines. It is now the norm to use just one space between sentences. Print on one side of the paper only.

On the first page of the manuscript, type your name, address, telephone number and email address (plus website or blog address if you have one) single spaced in the top left hand corner.

In the top right hand corner put the approximate number of words (rounded off), "Short Story", and the rights offered (e.g. "First British Serial Rights" or "First North American Serial Rights" etc.), single spaced. Do not put a copyright symbol as editors regard this as the sign of a novice. Do not number the first page.

About a third of the way down the page, type the title of your story (centred), skip a line and type "by" with your name (by-line).

Skip four lines (two double spaces) and start typing your story.

Succeeding pages should show your last name, title of your story and page number (e.g. Knowles-Daisies-2) in the top right unless the guidelines say otherwise. This can be done (in your

Word doc) by clicking on "Insert", "Page Numbers", "Top of page", "Alignment – Right". I deselect "Show number on first page".

I then insert my last name and the title of my story in front of the number. If somehow the number has wound up on the left side, I just click on it to highlight it, tab the number further to the right, then insert the words in front of it. You may still have to move it all to the right as far as it will go. No number will show on the first page.

Articles

Basically, the same procedures as above. Follow writers' guidelines for individual publications.

Book manuscripts

Cover page: Single space name, address, phone number, email address and web or blog address at top left; top right - single space description (e.g. Novel), genre and word count. Type the book title and your by-line (your name or pen name) half way down the page. Next page - start your first chapter. Centre chapter number and title a third of the way down the page. Insert a page break at the end of each chapter and make sure each chapter starts on a new page ("Insert" >> "break" >> "page break" in Microsoft Word).

Number each page from the second page on, starting with page 1. In Microsoft Word click "Insert" >> "Page numbers". Then select "position" and "alignment". I choose top right. Click "Format" and select zero for "start at". Do not check "show number on first page".

I then insert my last name and title of the book in front of the page number.

Poems

Usually no need to query. Check individual guidelines, but general rules are:-

- One poem per page.
- Put your name, address, phone number and email address, single spaced, in upper left hand corner.
- Type double spaced.
- If the poem continues on succeeding pages, attach the pages with a paper clip (do not staple).

Screenplays/Scripts

Usual query letter. Check individual guidelines. General rules are:-

- Submit your script in a binder.
- Usually divided into 3 - 6 acts.

For more information, check out "The Complete Book of Scriptwriting" by J. Michael Straczynski, or similar.

Online publications

Queries and submissions are similar to print publications.

- Check online guidelines.
- In the case of queries, only send attachments if guidelines allow; otherwise submit in body of email.

- Use your "sig" (signature) at the end of a query or cover letter, e.g.

  Your name
  Your email address
  Website or blog link if you have them
  You may also add your address and phone number.

Rights

"All Rights":

Just what it says. You've sold all rights to a publication and without its permission can never sell the work to another publication.

Remember my first short story to be accepted, a satirical story about a dentist, published in a tyre magazine? I was so excited about being published and getting paid for my story that I signed a form giving away All Rights.

"First Serial Rights":

Permission to publish your work for the first time in that particular publication. This can be further defined as "First North American Serial Rights" or "First British Serial Rights", etc.

"One Time Rights":

Permission to publish your work one time.

"Second Serial Rights":

Permission to republish a work.

"Subsidiary Rights":

Rights leading from publishing rights, such as in the movie industry.

Copyright

This is something that perplexes many new writers and even some that have been in the business for a long time. If you place a copyright symbol on your work when submitting to a publisher, the editor will usually consider that the sign of a novice. It is generally asserted that your copyright is automatically protected when your work is fixed by you in any tangible medium of expression.

If you wish to register your copyright, you can do so for a fee at the copyright department of the United States Library of Congress (contact them at https://copyright.gov), but that can become costly if you register the copyright of everything you write!

The business side of Queries and Submissions

- Keep track of your queries, submissions, rejections and acceptances. Some writers use computerized spread sheets. As mentioned previously, I use table grids ("Insert Table" grid in Microsoft Word).
- If your work is published and you haven't received payment within a reasonable space of time, send an invoice to the publication.

In a nutshell

There you have it all in a "nutshell"! I can only give you the basics though. You might want to consider purchasing "Formatting & Submitting Your Manuscript" by Cynthia Laufenberg and the Editors of Writer's Digest Books . It's "an easy-to-use guide, with dozens of charts, lists, models and sidebars showing what you need to know to submit your work correctly and enhance your chance of being published."

Above all, "keep it simple". Editors have stacks of queries and submissions to plough through.

You should hear back from reputable publications or publishers. However, after a reasonable length of time (or whatever time frame they give in their guidelines), if you haven't had a response, follow up with them. Don't be too disappointed though if you never hear back from some of them. Pick yourself up, dust yourself off and try other publications/publishers.

Don't give up!

It can take hours at a time to get your submissions out there, because editors, publishers and agents have so many different submission requirements (I once had to reformat the first three chapters of my novel to send to a certain publisher, as I discovered they required the first line of each new paragraph to be indented 0.3" instead of the default 0.5").

Remember, even if you're not successful right away, you WILL get better and better at your craft.

Good luck and happy submitting!

CHAPTER 11
REJECTIONS

IF you're a writer with a pile of rejections, pat yourself on the back! This means you have been getting your work out there and that you will probably achieve more success than those who hide their work in a drawer.

You can reduce rejections if you:-

- Study the markets and their guidelines. It's no good submitting a thousand word article or story if the publication requires 2,000+. And a magazine for seniors isn't going to be interested in a short story about cheerleaders and a high school football team!
- Query first if the publication requires it.
- Don't submit a topic that's already been covered (e.g. many magazines have story titles in back issues on their web site).
- Submit clean, typed copy, to the correct specifications and format, and enclose a stamped self-addressed envelope if you want your work sent back and/or a reply. Also, make sure there are sufficient stamps on

your outgoing envelope or it may be returned to you by the post office for insufficient postage. The same applies to return postage.

- Make sure your work is the very best it can be before you send it off – edit, edit, edit! Chop, chop, chop! Check it thoroughly and do "spell and grammar check" on your computer. Even if you have a good grasp of English grammar, "spell and grammar check" can pick up typos.
- Don't assume because a publication accepted several pieces of your work five years ago, they'll jump at your latest submission. Style, needs and editors often change.
- Take note of any constructive criticism from editors.
- After a rejection, immediately send the work out again to another market.

Some of the successful authors who received umpteen rejections before getting published are:-

John Creasy (774 rejections before selling his first story).

Alex Haley (200 rejections before "Roots").

Jack Canfield and Mark Victor Hansen ("Chicken Soup for the Soul" turned down by 33 publishers before it became a best seller and then a successful series).

Mary Higgins Clark (40 rejections before selling her first story).

Dr. Seuss (his first book was rejected 24 times).

Louis L'Amour (200 rejections before he sold his first novel).

Norman Mailer ("The Naked and the Dead" was rejected 12 times).

And we've all heard how F. Scott Fitzgerald papered his bedroom walls with rejection slips before he eventually sold a story!

Just remember - rejection does not equal failure!

CHAPTER 12
GETTING PAID

I DON'T believe in writing for free! Even if payment for a piece is comparatively low, this proves my work has been selected on merit by the publication. I do make exceptions to this belief, though:

- I occasionally write non paying articles to promote worthy causes or to help people in need.
- With press releases for business establishments, the publications don't pay me, but my client does. And if I submit the press releases in the form of a feature story, I usually get a by-line (handy for future clips). I've also heard that some journalists have received payment from the newspaper they submit their press release to as well. I have never tried this though. I'm just happy with another by-line.

You may love to write and you may be good at it, but you should work hard at producing the very best piece of work that you can. Never be content with second best.

I know, it's tempting to click the save button on your computer, print out your work, and dash it off to a publisher, but stop! Have you checked the grammar and spelling? Have you deleted every superfluous word?

Don't think it's easy to get paid as a writer. To be considered a professional writer, submit your work in a professional manner.

Record your submissions and if your work is accepted, make a note of the date. Give the publication a decent period of time (about a month if the publication is local; longer if overseas). Then if you haven't received a cheque, send them an invoice. Of course, estimated response time is often listed in submission guidelines.

Invoices

This is the format I use for invoices:-

Centre your name, address, telephone number(s) and email address at the top of plain white 8 ½"x 11" good quality paper (with a little personal logo if you wish):

Date:

Invoice #: ....

[This is helpful to the accounting department and if it's your first invoice, start at #101, so you don't look like a newbie!]

To: [Title of your work (not the publication's name) and date of publication] $................. [insert amount if you know what they're paying; if not, leave this blank]

Thank you.

[not necessary to sign the invoice]

[Often, the publication will also require your social security number or equivalent, depending on where you live].

Cover letters

Include a cover letter too, if you wish:-

Centre your name, address, etc., as above

Date:...........................

Dear [insert Editor's name],

Thank you for using my [insert "article", "story", etc., as appropriate] in your [insert date of issue] issue.I would be grateful if you would kindly forward the enclosed invoice to your accounting department.

It has been a pleasure writing for your publication and I look forward to submitting more ....[insert "articles", "stories", etc., as appropriate] in the future for your consideration.

Yours sincerely,

[sign your name]

[print your name]

Rates

Writers' rates of pay vary considerably. Some new publications with low budgets only pay small amounts or in complimentary copies. Others pay by the word or in set amounts for specific word counts.

Publications'/Publishers' Submission Guidelines usually state rates of pay or royalties.

Many online markets pay little or nothing, but with the ever-evolving opportunities on the Internet, it's a great way for writers' work to get noticed.

Kill Fees

A "kill fee" is an amount sometimes offered by publications to established writers on assignment, in case another more important story comes along that they need to use or a competitor publishes a similar story (or for whatever other reason).

If a publication decides not to use the assigned piece, the author can be paid a kill fee. In some cases, this is negotiable in advance.

Many writers dislike kill fees, which are often considered too low. Of course, when a kill fee is paid, the author immediately has the right to offer the work elsewhere.

Making a living at writing

Some of us are fortunate enough to make a living at writing; most of us need a "day job" as well. But getting paid is not only what writing is all about.

Experiencing the flow of creativity from a well of inspiration; the satisfaction of a well crafted piece of work; and communicating across barriers - these are some of the reasons we write. And if a nice fat cheque arrives in the mail too, that just puts the icing on the cake!

CHAPTER 13
PROMOTIONAL WRITING

PROMOTIONAL writing (Public Relations work) can be fun, provide additional income and if you write it well, you may get a by-line.

My first introduction to this aspect of writing was when I ditched a well paid secretarial job to jump-start my writing career. But I didn't have a PLAN! I only received one response to my small classified ad and that was from an acquaintance! This was before the wonderful age of the Internet though.

Grateful for the assignment, I threw myself wholeheartedly into my friend's short-term project, writing the text for his villa and car rental brochures.

Most of the local PR market at that time seemed to be swallowed up by a couple of established writers with their own agencies.

Then I heard that a local shopping mall needed a writer and I rushed there, with clips, pen and note pad in hand, to meet the marketing manager.

This began an exciting year of interviewing storeowners for feature stories, covering mall events and assisting with seasonal promotions. I used my cheap little camera (this was before digitals) and clambered all over the mall taking photos of proprietors, customers and events.

Leading up to Christmas, I was asked to write a story for a colouring book, to be given out to customers' children. I complied with a light-hearted tale about a parrot. A staff member did the illustrations and the kids loved it!

Another pasture for promotional writing is the large number of restaurants that want short pieces submitted to the local press, to attract customers to their eateries.

I wrote a few of these articles, attempting to make each restaurant sound more of an interesting place to eat than a list of what was on the menu. One title was "Le Shack lives on - and your grandmother will love it!" It was about a casual restaurant on Nassau's harbour "where you could bring the kids, the dogs and your grandmother!"

You can write articles for almost any business or organization and submit them to the media as press releases.

The highlight of my PR work occurred when a local shipping agency asked me to write about Royal Caribbean Cruise Lines. My husband and I got to go on a complimentary five day Caribbean cruise, so I could write about Royal Caribbean first hand! I spent most of the time running all over the ship, taking photos and doing interviews, while Erskine relaxed and enjoyed the amenities!

Erskine is a guitarist and vocalist, so imagine his delight when we got a chance to meet Mary Wilson, former Lead Singer of the Supremes (before Diana Ross), who was performing on the ship!

Afterwards, I submitted my articles to the local newspapers and also sent a copy of the main article to the cruise line for them to use in their marketing.

Now, that assignment was really fun!

THE NUTS AND BOLTS OF PR

Have a plan! Write down:

- The name of your business (just use your own name if you like).
- Your slogan if you have one (e.g. "Putting YOUR business first through the media").
- Your mission statement (e.g. "Promoting clients' services through the media in a professional and timely manner").
- Your goal (e.g. To become the top PR person in your town).

Plan your marketing strategy

Newspaper advertisements, radio spots, direct mail, web site, newsletters, social media, etc. (keep it simple and don't spend too much money to start with).

Chat up your editors

After the press release is printed, give the editors a quick call (they're busy people) or email them, to thank them for using the piece. Thank them for the by-line too if they gave you one.

Know your locals

Know your local newspapers and their writing style. Specially format your story for each one.

For one newspaper, I'd submit the full story and they usually printed the whole article.

For another, I'd submit the full story, but with a different opening and ending. Again, they'd print the full version.

For a local tabloid, I'd edit the story until it was short and "punchy".

And for the fourth publication, I'd edit and slant the story towards their youth column.

I'd also submit different photos for each publication.

Submitting a press release

Submit your press release to the media, just as you would a regular submission, but type "Press Release" and "For Immediate Release" at top left.

- Submitting hard copy to publications – double space.
- Submitting to Radio and television – triple space.

CHAPTER 14
SELF-PUBLISHING OR TRADITIONAL

AT one time, I must admit, I was doubtful about self-publishing. I felt my work would only have true worth if it were accepted by a traditional publisher. However, that is easier said than done! Of course, it would be marvellous if we could all receive that eagerly awaited phone call from a top publishing house, informing us that they loved our book and would be sending us a hefty advance.

There are millions of books out there in the world, and traditional publishers receive endless book proposals. How can our books stand out amongst all of the competition?

Amazon has opened up a whole new era for self-published authors. We must do our marketing though. And even if you are traditionally published, the publishers often expect you to do your own share of the marketing for your book.

I finally converted over to self-publishing when a retired and well respected editor that I know set up a publishing firm online to publish his own books, along with a selection of high calibre books that had impressed him. He was in effect self-publishing ("print on demand"). He told me he didn't have endless years left in his life to keep submitting his books to traditional publishers.

That's when it hit me. I was in the same boat. I had written a novel and submitted it to around seventy traditional publishers and literary agents without any success. How many years would it take me to be accepted? Would I still be alive?!

I had intended to keep on trying until my novel submissions had reached one hundred, at which time I MIGHT consider self-publishing. However, I had self-published my book "Sunbeams from the Heart – A Collection of Twelve Romantic Short Stories" on Amazon and sales were going well.

I therefore stopped submitting my novel to traditional publishers and agents and self-published my mystery romance novel "Love at Sunset" (now titled Dangerous Devotion") on Amazon as well!

I use Amazon.com (KDP) for my e-books and paperbacks. I could publish with a print on demand publisher (at a cost), who would probably list my books on their website. However, with Amazon being one of the largest retailers in the world, books get great exposure with them. Purchasers pay by credit card and the royalties are sent to the author's bank account.

Sometimes I also upload my books to Smashwords.com and if they are approved for premium distribution, they are sent out to major online retailers such as Barnes & Noble, Kobo and Apple. You can only do this if you have NOT selected KDP Select when you publish your e-book on Amazon.

E-book publishing on Amazon

Once purchased, e-books are downloaded to customers' Kindles. For those of you who don't have a Kindle, no problem. The free Kindle app can be downloaded from Amazon for most major smart phones, tablets and computers.

Paperback publishing

I have had some considerable success with publishing and selling my paperbacks on Amazon. When I order author discounted copies of my books, they always arrive well packed and in excellent condition.

The cost

If you learn how to format your books and design your own book covers, it won't cost you anything to publish your books on Amazon. If you're not into graphic design, you could hire an expert. You will need to market your books though and there will be a cost for that, depending on how much marketing you do.

Royalties

Royalties for publishing on Amazon are minimal, but the easy and affordable submission process makes it quite cost effective.

Unfortunately, the "tax man" still gets a cut from your royalties (in most countries in the world, I believe)! I publish through the American Amazon.com so I have to pay tax to the IRS. The tax and Amazon's fee are taken out before I receive the balance of my royalties.

The future

I plan to continue publishing my books on Amazon. Of course, that doesn't prevent a top publishing house from noticing one of my books one day and approaching me with a six figure deal!

CHAPTER 15
THE POWER OF THE PEN

SINCE the beginning of time, words have empowered writers. From the symbols and pictures of our prehistoric ancestors to the printed pages from our modern computers, we have always expressed ourselves in some form of the written word.

In mediaeval England, Town Criers, dressed in colourful livery and reading from parchment scrolls, shouted out important news and events to eager townspeople, most of whom couldn't read or write.

And Associated Press bureau chief Terry Anderson, kidnapped by Shiites in Lebanon during the eighties and held hostage for almost seven years, kept himself sane while in prison, by writing thirty-two poems "in his head" and memorizing them!

On the day his fellow hostages, Terry Waite and Thomas Sutherland, were released, Anderson was given pen, paper and one hour to write. He scribbled down eleven of his memorized poems for the freed prisoners to take to his wife.

Dr. Ben Carson came from a broken home in the black ghettos of Detroit. As a boy, he had a fierce temper, bad grades and low self-esteem. When he nearly failed the fifth grade, his mother, who'd had a limited education, sent Ben and his brother to the public library on a regular basis. She demanded that they read two books a week and limit their television viewing. Mrs. Carson also made the boys turn in book reports to her.

At first, Ben resented his mother's new rules! Then he came to realize that through books, he could go anywhere in the world and do anything he desired.

Dr. Ben Carson became Director of Paediatric Neurosurgery at John Hopkins University Hospital, Baltimore, USA, and is considered one of the world's top brain surgeons. He uses the "power of the pen" himself to encourage and inspire others. His books "Gifted Hands", "Think Big" and "The Big Picture" made the bestseller lists.

"The power of the pen" can educate, entertain, encourage, inform, persuade, proclaim, help, guide or inspire. Words can soothe us or excite us; make us happy or sad; romantic or bitter; remember the past or look to the future; drive us into battle or make us stand up for peace.

Sadly, the "power of the pen" can also be used in harmful ways. Terrorists have learned from evil manuals how to maim and kill; cults twist the words of the Bible to entrap new members; some links on the Internet lead the innocent to pornography, sadism and hatred.

But in general, the positive words of writers, past and present, far outweigh the negative.

However you use your gift of writing, use it wisely, for YOU have the "Power of the Pen"!

Good luck with your writing projects. I wish you much success, as there is nothing like the joy of writing and getting published.

If you enjoyed **How to Be the Best Writer Ever,**
your comments online would be greatly
appreciated. Please feel free to leave
a review on Amazon or elsewhere.

Thank you

Join our **Mailing List** to receive notifications of all new releases
by Fay Knowles! It's quick & easy. Sign up at
tinyurl.com/y6mw5zuw.

85

OTHER BOOKS BY FAY KNOWLES

(ORDER ON AMAZON)

SUNBEAMS FROM THE HEART:

A COLLECTION OF TWELVE ROMANTIC SHORT STORIES:

A beautiful keepsake. Love themes in this delightful collection of romantic short stories tell of nostalgia, bright new beginnings, homecoming, second chances - and the unexpected! Heart-warming stories that propel you on a journey through Scotland, England, The Bahamas and rural America.

Available on Amazon as an e-book and in paperback.

DANGEROUS DEVOTION - Book 1 in the Buchanan Mystery Romance Series:

"A MOVING TALE OF FAMILY DYNAMICS AND RELATIONSHIPS IN LATER LIFE -" - JUANITA COULSON, BOOKS EDITOR, "THE LADY" MAGAZINE, U.K.

Greed, jealousy, family secrets, bitter grudges and forbidden love!

If your relationship was threatened, what lengths would you go to in order to save it? Facing imminent danger and fierce opposition to love a second time around, Violet and Gordon seek a new life in Gordon's homeland of Scotland, thousands of miles away from where they had lived in Nassau, Bahamas, but trouble catches up with them in their little loch side cottage.

In the meantime, back in Nassau an unscrupulous attorney appears on the scene, along with a crooked realtor. What they do and the extent they would go to leads to a shocking ending. Set in The Bahamas and Scotland, with scenes also in Fort Lauderdale, New York, London and Devon.

A stand-alone mystery-romance, based on Fay Knowles' short story "Love at Sunset", first published in "The Lady" magazine, London, England, and which also appears in her short story collection "Sunbeams from The Heart: A Collection of Twelve Romantic Short Stories".

Available on Amazon as an e-book and in paperback.

For "Deadly Deceit In Paradise", Book Two in the Buchanan Mystery Romance Series (another stand-alone novel), go to amazon.com/dp/B0863V6HHJ

And Join Fay's Mailing List to be notified when the Buchanan Mystery Romance Series Book 3 has been released: tinyurl.com/y6mw5zuw

DEADLY DECEIT IN PARADISE - Book 2 in the Buchanan Mystery Romance Series:

A mysterious death in paradise leads a young woman down a path that will determine her future.

Natalie Barrett flies from London to Nassau, Bahamas, to attend a favourite uncle's funeral and the reading of his will. While staying at her deceased uncle's home, she notices a string of suspicious events that lead her to believe he may not have died from natural causes as reported. Will her curiosity and subsequent amateur investigation point to murder? And will she have to choose between the two handsome men she meets?

A stand alone novel filled with intrigue, romance, scandal and mystery that will keep your mind on it long after you've read the last page.

Available on Amazon as an e-book and in paperback.

For "Dangerous Devotion" (Book 1 in the Buchanan Mystery Romance Series) go to amazon.co.uk/dp/B01EVYUSAC

And join Fay's Mailing List to be notified when the Buchanan Mystery Romance Series Book 3 has been released: tinyurl.com/y6mw5zuw

published in "The Lady" magazine, London, U.K., and "The Broadkill Review", Delaware, U.S.A.

"What a marvellous collection of stories. They will reel you in, entertain and refresh you, and have you eager to go on to the next one!" - Amazon Customer

Available on Amazon as an e-book and in paperback.

Fascinating Scottish Memorabilia - The Scottish Connection contains a wealth of information - Scottish ancestry, historical facts, genealogy, comparable 1978 prices, geographical descriptions, personal anecdotes, nostalgia and precious old photos.

"Driving long distances in a short space of time throughout the United Kingdom is the norm nowadays. However, in the seventies it was often an adventure to cover the length or breadth of Britain."

In this illustrated mini-memoir Stirling-born Fay Knowles shares memories of her 1978 journey back to Scotland with her mother and young sons, to revisit their Scottish roots."

Available on Amazon as an e-book and in paperback.

FUNNELS is a poignant short story about a young woman who longs to escape her dreary, hard working existence on a Caribbean

island. With a baby daughter and irresponsible casino dealer husband, she is tied down to eking a living working tables in a local restaurant. When an opportunity suddenly presents itself, she is torn between her family and the prospect of elevating herself

Connect with Fay Knowles at:
https://fayknowles.blogspot.com

facebook.com/faykwrites
twitter.com/faykwrites
instagram.com/faykwrites
linkedin.com/in/fayknowles